D1530934

YOU WANT ME TO BE GOOD ALL DAY?

and other prayers for children

BiG
AL

YOU WANT ME TO BE GOOD ALL DAY?

and other prayers for children

BY FR. JOE KEMPF
WITH BIG AL

illustrated by Chris Sharp

Liguori
LIGUORI, MISSOURI

Imprimi Potest:
Thomas D. Picton, C.Ss.R.
Provincial, Denver Province
The Redemptorists

Published by Liguori Publications
Liguori, Missouri 63057, USA
To order, call 800-325-9521.
www.liguori.org

ISBN 978-0-7648-1843-1

Liguori Publications, a nonprofit corporation, is an apostolate of the
Redemptorists. To learn more about the Redemptorists, visit Redemptorists.com.

Printed and assembled in Mexico
13 12 11 10 09   5 4 3 2 1
First edition

What's Inside...

Introduction

You might know my big brother.
Big Al is his name.
I'm the "little sister."
Annie is my name.

Sometimes I do annoy him,
though mostly I am nice.
(If Big Al heard me say that,
he'd probably roll his eyes.)

Deep down we love each other
'cause that's what families do,
the families we grow up with
and all God's people, too.

We hope inside this little book
that you and God will meet,
so you might hear that "You are loved,"
'cause that's how we're complete.

You Want Me to Be Good ALL DAY?

You want me to be good ALL DAY?
You must be kidding me.
It's not that I don't want to, God.
It's just so hard, You see.

I'll do okay for quite a while,
but then things fall apart.
That's when I need to think of You
and make a brand new start.

For though I am not perfect
(and I will never be),
even in the worst of times,
You're there loving me.

You call me to begin again
and remember that it's true
that I'll be truly happy
when I am most like You.

Dear God, I Had a Dream Last Night

Dear God, I had a dream last night.
I woke up so afraid,
but when I looked I saw that it
was just the bed unmade.

There was no monster after all,
and there will never be.
Instead all through my every night,
You're there loving me.

"Do I Still Fit Inside Your Heart?"

"Do I still fit inside your heart?"
I asked my mom one day.
"You see that I am bigger now,
in oh so many ways."

"There's always room for you," Mom said,
"however big you'll be.
You'll always be my precious child.
You mean so much to me."

I'm glad that You're like that, oh God.
Your heart's so big and free
that even when I'm all grown up,
You'll still have room for me.

A big
heart!

I Gave My Dog a Haircut

I gave my dog a haircut.
Now Mom is mad at me.
It seemed a good idea,
but turned out not to be.

Mom said I should "use my head"
and try to think things through.
That doesn't always work so well.
You understand, don't You?

Loving Jesus, please help me
to do the best I can,
and when things don't turn out so well,
to learn and try again.

Bad idea.

Did Jesus Have to Take a Bath?

"Did Jesus have to take a bath?"
I asked my mom one day.
(I was trying to get out of mine
and couldn't find a way.)

Dear Jesus, I will never know
all that You had to do.
I'm sure that You did many things
Your mother asked of You.

All through Your life,
You helped the world
in times both hard and fun.
Jesus, help me be like You
and do what must be done.

Someday She'll Take Communion, God

Someday she'll take Communion, God,
as others get to do.
She wonders what she'll then be like
or what things she might do.

She thinks that she'll glow in the dark,
but I know that's not true.
Instead, there's something better.
You'll help her be like You.

Amen!

I Know I'm Not Alone Right Now

I know I'm not alone right now,
though I appear to be,
for when we pray, we all are one.
There's more here than I see.

I join with people everywhere.
They're in this prayer somehow,
and everyone in heaven
is here with me right now.

I Lift These Hands to You, Oh God

I lift these hands to You, oh God.
You see how small they are,
and with Your help, they'll do great things,
'cause that's what they are for.

Please bless these hands for goodness.
May they do right, not wrong.
These hands are for Your work, dear God.
My hands to You belong.

Bless these hands.

She Was Kind to Me Today

She was kind to me today
when others turned their heads.
I could have felt so lonely;
I felt Your love instead.

I thank You for her goodness, God.
She helped me know You care.
Her simple act of kindness
showed that You were there.

It's good to be kind.

Not Every Kid Looks Quite Like Me

Not every kid looks quite like me.
I think that is so fun,
'cause inside each and every child,
we see the good You've done.

For when You made us each, oh God,
You did so with great joy,
and You put some of YOU inside
of every girl and boy.

You love
us all!

My Aunt Is Getting Married

My aunt is getting married, God.
It's wonderful to see.
They'll promise love forever,
yet how hard that must be!

In good times and in bad times,
through laughter and through tears,
forever they will choose to love
through each and every year.

But that's how You love us, oh God,
in good times and in bad.
Your love is always with us.
That makes my heart so glad!

Love
always.

I Didn't Mean to Break the Lamp

I didn't mean to break the lamp.
It was an accident.
But Mom's still kind of mad at me.
Straight to my room I went!

I could have been more careful,
though accidents aren't sins.
It's when we're mean on purpose
that no one ever wins.

But You are so forgiving, God,
with love You hold me tight,
and when I'm truly sorry,
You help me make things right.

Oops.

GLUE

What Will I Be When I Grow Up?

"What will I be when I grow up?"
people have asked me.
I do not know the answer.
There's so much I could be.

But there's another question
that my dad asks of me.
The question is not WHAT, it's HOW:
"Tell me HOW you'll be."

He says what matters most to You
is not what I will do.
It's HOW I'll live my every day.
Will I be kind like You?

Help the world!

Coach Says He's Embarrassed

Coach says he's embarrassed, God.
We didn't win today.
We made mistakes and lost the game,
but don't they call it "play"?

I want to win; You know I do.
I also want to play.
Winning isn't everything.
"Stop," I want to say.

"Please let us just be children."
It's one thing Coach could choose.
Help us know that we are loved,
even when we lose.

It's just
a game.

My Brother Got a Special Gift

My brother got a special gift.
It's for his special day.
I wish that I weren't jealous
and didn't feel this way.

You want me to be glad for him.
Please help me, Lord, to see
that when he gets a blessing,
there's no less love for me.

'Cause everything I really need
is right here in my heart.
I am loved and I can love.
That's where true joy will start.

It's hard
for me.

Often When It's Time for Prayer

Often when it's time for prayer,
I don't know what to say.
It seems that others know great words,
but I can't really pray.

When I don't know which words to use,
I know it's still okay,
for when I do the best I can,
You hear what I can't say.

Help me
Pray.

Grandpa's feeling sick, dear God.
Everyone is scared.
They wonder if he'll be okay,
and so I make this prayer.

God, send Your love and healing peace
to flow through him today.
Please let him know that You're right there.
With all my heart, I pray.

I pray for
Grandpa.

Get Well
Soon!

Tomorrow I've Got School Again

Tomorrow I've got school again.
On some days, school is fun.
Tomorrow won't be one of them:
My homework's still not done.

Help me become wiser, God,
in many different ways.
Please help me to keep growing
and learning all my days.

Homework!

Loving Father, Bless This House

Loving Father, bless this house
and all who in it live.
May our home be filled with love.
Help us to forgive.

May all who ever visit us
find blessings when they're here.
Fill this home with goodness, Lord,
Your presence ever near.

This Prayer Is From the Both of Us

This prayer is from the both of us
as we now end this day.
Today was filled with many things,
and now we want to pray.

We both can be annoying, God,
but now that day is done,
we turn to You together
and join our hearts as one.

Thank You for the gifts You gave.
Forgive us for our sins,
and help us know that when we wake
a whole new chance begins.

We love
You!

CD TRACK LISTING